SO-CQQ-831

The Take-It-Easy Good-Times Cookbook

Easy, Economical, Exciting Entrees

Patricia B. Mitchell

Copyright © 1991 by Patricia B. Mitchell. All rights reserved.

Portions of this manuscript were originally published under the title *A Month of Magnificent Main Dishes*, copyright © 1987, 1989 by Patricia B. Mitchell.

Published 1991 by the author.
 Mail: Mitchells, P.O. Box 429, Chatham, VA 24531
 Book Sales: 800-967-2867
 E-mail: *Answers@FoodHistory.com*
 Websites: *FoodHistory.com* and *MitchellsPublications.com*

Compact Edition
Printed in the U.S.A.
ISBN-10: 0-925117-51-X
ISBN-13: 978-0-925117-51-9

Third Printing, January 2014

- *Illustrations* -

All illustrations are adapted from images provided by Dover Publications, Inc., New York.

The cover design is by Sarah E. Mitchell, *VintageDesigns.com*.

Table of Contents

My Philosophy of Cooking

Some people routinely spend hours each day on meal preparation. Especially in our travels in Europe we encountered cooking which has been elevated to an art. The pâtés, terrines, and complex sauces of France; the skillfully-prepared soups and pasta dishes of Italy; the multi-step preparation of such Greek dishes as moussaka and baklava are impressive (and most enjoyable to eat!). Yet I will admit that I seldom spend the kitchen time necessary to create such fancy cuisine. I once read a quote in which the lady said, "I don't want to spend my life stuffing mushrooms."

I concur. As much as I love good food, I also enjoy spending time with my family, reading, writing, walking, traveling, etc. Therefore I do not go into the kitchen at 2 p.m. to begin dinner. About 5 p.m. is the time I usually start to fix supper. (Of course if homemade bread or a cake or something like that is on the menu that will have to be done ahead of time.)

Yet, despite the fact I do not often produce labor-intensive gourmet meals, I adore cooking. I surmise that you do, too, or you would not be reading a "chatty" cookbook. — One reporter who was writing a story about my cookbook business began the article by contrasting my style of meal preparation with that of some moderns who "nuke a burrito in the microwave." Anyway, to get to my point, if you do not like to cook at all even an hour spent cooking is a bore. If you are an epicurean, endless hours invested in a dish are worthwhile. If you are like me (busy) but fond of delicious food, minimal preparation time is the ideal.

The following recipes are uncomplicated, economical dishes. They utilize simple preparation techniques, a limited number of standard ingredients, and they taste delicious. Because I like to "interact" with my food as it cooks (stirring, studying, sampling), I do not use a microwave oven. Because my family and I are health-conscious I do not use a lot of convenience foods or mixes — which often contain excess fats, salt, sugar, and chemicals. Those, then, are the parameters of this volume: no junk, no tricks. Famed 18th-century London writer of *The Art of Cookery, Made Plain and Easy*, Hannah Glasse, intoned suspiciously, "If gentlemen will have French cooks, they must pay for French tricks." — I reiterate: I love French cuisine, when time permits! In *this* book, though, expect easy recipes, and an outcome of satisfying meals. The fun of cooking, and then the pleasure of dining with family or friends inevitably equals good times . . . .

Spoonburgers

Henry and I eloped at a young age, and then set up housekeeping in Blacksburg, Virginia, where we were attending Virginia Polytechnic Institute ("V.P.I.," now generally known as "Virginia Tech"). At that time, in the late 1960's, Blacksburg was still very much a quaint mountain town. One local business we patronized was a main-street, antiquated structure known as the Blue Grass Market. In those days ground beef — they just called it "hamburger meat" — was often only 29 cents a pound. When you make the following recipe I doubt that you can even find ground beef for as little as $1.29 per pound!

* * *

$^1/_2$ lb. lean ground beef, crumbled, cooked, and drained
$^1/_2$ c. onion, chopped
$^1/_2$ c. celery, chopped
1 can condensed tomato soup

After preparing the meat, put it and the other ingredients into the skillet, stir and cover. Simmer 10 to 15 minutes, stirring occasionally. (If the mixture is too thick, add a little water.) Serve hot over split and warmed hamburger buns. Serves 3 or 4.

Habana Cabana Black Bean Soup

After college came a brief stint in the Air Force during which time Henry was assigned to bases in Biloxi, Mississippi, and Dayton, Ohio — our world was widening! Gulf Coast food was an awakening to our palates. In fact, exploring the lovely Gulf Coast area and Louisiana sharpened all our senses and expanded our minds and experience. Dayton, too, brought new circumstances and friends, and dining adventures. Thanks to one Air Force couple we met in Dayton we eventually made the acquaintance of black beans, a Caribbean staple. (Jane Cox served us Black Beans and Rice.) These velvety, midnight-dark beans are a delicious addition to any diet.

* * *

1 lb. black beans
8 c. water
1 lg. onion, chopped
1 lg. garlic clove, minced
$^1/_2$ tsp. salt
$^1/_4$ tsp. black pepper
1 (15-oz.) can tomato sauce

Sort and rinse beans. Soak overnight; then bring to a boil. Reduce heat and cook for one to two hours, or until tender. Add remaining ingredients and simmer another hour. Add more salt and pepper if needed, and serve.

The next two potato-ey soups are true "comfort foods."

"Essence of Meat & Potatoes" Soup

3 sm. potatoes, peeled and chopped
$^1/_2$ c. onion, chopped
6 c. water
$^3/_4$ tsp. salt
$^1/_4$ tsp. black pepper
2 beef bouillon cubes (or chicken bouillon cubes if you're not
        the "meat and potatoes" type)
1 $^1/_2$ c. dry milk powder
$^1/_2$ to 1 tsp. oregano
1 $^1/_2$ c. instant mashed potato flakes

Put the potatoes, onion, and water in a large pot, bring to a boil, then reduce the heat and simmer 15 to 20 minutes or until the potatoes are tender. Add salt, pepper, and 2 beef or chicken bouillon cubes. Stir well. Add 1½ c. dry milk powder and the oregano, stirring to make all of the milk powder dissolve. Just before serving, stir in 1½ c. instant mashed potato flakes. If the soup is too thick, pour in additional hot water.

Fast Chick Potato Soup

4 c. chicken broth
4 c. milk
2 tsp. onion powder
½ tsp. (or more) salt
¼ tsp. black pepper
2 c. dry instant potato flakes

Heat the broth and milk to boiling. Reduce heat and stir in the other ingredients. Simmer a few minutes and serve.

Hot tips for hot soups: To create delightful one-of-a-kind soups, keep a large plastic container labeled "For Soup" in your freezer. When you have a bit of leftover casserole, rice, pasta, vegetables, or vegetable cooking liquid, pour these goodies into the container. (Obviously, you should not put anything in it like extra fruit salad or cold scrambled eggs — you want to end up with a compatible group of ingredients in the potage!) When the container is full, thaw out the mixture, heat it up, and simmer awhile. If necessary, add water to thin. Season to taste with salt, pepper, and a favorite condiment such as Texas Pete, Tabasco, or Worcestershire sauce. Garlic powder will also boost the flavor, as will other herbs that you enjoy.

Florentine Fish Stew

Technically speaking, according to *Larousse Gastronomique*, "Florentine" refers to a method of food preparation involving fish or eggs which are set on a bed of cooked and buttered spinach, covered with Mornay sauce, sprinkled with grated cheese, and then browned. For the purpose of naming this recipe I took a little liberty, and christened it Florentine — it does contain spinach!

* * *

1 (28-oz.) can tomatoes, chopped, plus water to equal 4 cups
$1/2$ c. onion, chopped
1 (10-oz.) pkg. frozen chopped spinach
$1/2$ to 1 lb. frozen ocean perch fillets (or other fish of your choice)
1 c. ditalini (small pasta)
Salt and pepper
$1/4$ tsp. red pepper flakes

Take the spinach and fish out of the freezer about half an hour or so before you start fixing this dish. To begin, put the chopped tomatoes and their liquid into a large pot. Heat to boiling and add onion. Reduce heat slightly. With a big knife cut the partially thawed spinach and fish into small cubes.

Add to the simmering tomato mixture. Stir in the pasta, and cook 15 to 20 minutes or until the fish and pasta are done, adding additional water if the mixture gets too thick. Season to taste with salt and pepper and sprinkle with red pepper flakes. Makes approximately 6 servings, depending upon what else you are having.

Let me tell you a silly story about me and mustard. Henry has a short lunch break (but it's a blessing that he gets to come home to lunch at all — that's rare in this day and age). Anyway, I often find myself rushing around madly as lunchtime approaches. (I don't want to start preparations TOO early because that would cut short our home school time . . . .)

Anyway, one day I was fixing cheeseburgers. I had put mayo on the children's buns (that reads kind of funny!) and mustard on ours (we like 'em that way), and was returning those two jars to the refrigerator when the big jar of mustard slipped out of my hand! It did not break, but the lid was not screwed on tightly and when the bottom of the jar hit the floor, the lid shot off. Mustard flew everywhere — on schoolbooks, floor lamp shade, refrigerator, bookshelf, ceiling. A yellow mess. Cleaning up led to more trouble — a smashed metal cabinet top (it was not built to support the weight of a person); a blackened sweater sleeve — but that's another story!! Anyway, be cautious with the mustard in this recipe.

Ravioli & Beans

2 cans ravioli
2 cans red kidney beans *or* pintos
1 tbsp. spicy brown mustard
1 tsp. celery salt

Raw onion for garnish, chopped in rings

Heat together the first four ingredients in a pot on the stove. Before serving, add raw chopped onions or onion rings for a garnish. Serves 6 to 8, depending upon appetites.

Note: When I'm expecting I always crave ravioli!

Sausage Cheese Squares

This is a fabulous lunch dish!

* * *

2$^1/_2$ c. *Master Biscuit Mix** (see below)
$^1/_2$ tsp. sage
$^1/_4$ tsp. paprika
$^1/_2$ lb. crumbled, cooked, and drained sausage
1 onion, chopped

2 tbsp. vegetable oil
1 c. plain yogurt
1 1/3 c. milk
1 egg, beaten
1/2 to 1 c. grated American cheese

Mix the dry ingredients. Add remaining ingredients. Stir together, and spoon into a greased 8x8x2-inch Pyrex dish. Bake at 350° F. for around 45 minutes or until golden brown.

Master Biscuit Mix:

4 c. all-purpose flour
4 c. whole wheat flour
1/3 c. baking powder
1 tbsp. salt (or less, to suit taste)

Combine the above ingredients. Store in refrigerator or freezer.

Seaside Villa Tuna

Now for some easy main courses . . . . This "off-the-shelf" / "out of the freezer" recipe is tasty as well as visually attractive. Great when you haven't had time to go to the grocery store!

By the way, some people find it efficient and economical to shop only every two weeks. My family and I make such a food jaunt to a large chain food store to purchase staples — dry milk powder, peanut butter, molasses, oats, flour, and the like. We go to a locally owned and operated grocery store about every three or four days to keep supplied with perishables — fresh fruit and vegetables, etc.

* * *

1 or 2 cans cream of mushroom soup (I do use a lot of canned
        soups in my "short-cut" cooking!)
1/3 c. onion, chopped
1/4 c. milk
1 tbsp. lemon juice
Black pepper to taste

1 can tuna, water-packed, undrained
1½ c. green peas, fresh or frozen
½ c. Cheddar cheese, grated
¼ c. sherry
Paprika
Cooked rice (preferably brown)

Heat together the first five ingredients. Add the tuna, breaking it up slightly. In a few minutes add the peas and cheese. Stir in the sherry. Pour into a serving dish and dust with paprika. Serve cooked rice in a separate bowl and allow diners to heap some rice on their plates, and then spoon on the tuna mixture.

Beginner's Luck Tuna Loaf and Sauce

The mastery of this dish was one of my early culinary achievements back in Blacksburg. We still love it.

* * *

1½ c. soft bread crumbs
¾ c. milk
2 tbsp. sweet pickle, minced
1 egg, beaten
Dash of pepper
2 small cans of tuna *or* salmon, drained*
1 tbsp. lemon juice

Combine all ingredients. Grease a loaf pan, and pack the mixture into the pan. Bake at 350° F. for 30 to 40 minutes and serve with **sauce**:

2 tbsp. butter *or* margarine
2 tbsp. flour
¼ tsp. salt
*¼ c. liquid from canned tuna *or* salmon
¾ c. milk
2 tbsp. catsup

Melt butter, and blend in flour, stirring frequently for several minutes. Add salt, liquid from canned fish (if there is not enough, use extra milk), and the $3/4$ cup milk. Stir and cook until mixture is smooth and thick. Stir in catsup. Remove the tuna loaf from the oven and invert it on a platter. Pour the sauce over the tuna loaf and serve sliced. (It might crumble a little when you slice it, but that is O.K.)

Not-The-Usual Tuna / Green Pea Casserole

The flavor and bright green color of fresh or frozen peas enhance this casserole, and the tomatoes also add color as well as just a hint of tartness. This dish is deliciously saucy. My son David coined the word "sauce-erole" to describe this sort of recipe.

* * *

2 cans tuna, undrained
$1/2$ c. onion, chopped
1 can cream of mushroom soup
$1/2$ c. canned tomatoes, chopped and drained
1 c. fresh or frozen green peas, cooked
2 c. broad egg noodles, cooked
Cheddar cheese, grated

Into a saucepan pour the undrained tuna, and add onion. Cook slowly until the onion is tender. To this mixture add the remaining ingredients except for the cheese. Spoon into a two-quart casserole and bake at 400° F. for 20 minutes. Top with cheese and serve. Feeds four or five.

Chicken à la Peacock

This pea-speckled main dish is as pretty as a peacock! (Those colorful peas show up again!)

* * *

1 can cream of chicken soup
1 can cream of mushroom soup

$^1/_2$ c. milk
2 tbsp. ripe olives, chopped
2 tbsp. pimientos, chopped
Dash of black pepper

$1^1/_2$ c. cooked chicken, chopped
$1^1/_2$ c. fresh or frozen green peas

Hot cooked rice

Heat together the first six ingredients. When hot and bubbly, add the chicken and heat. Add the green peas, heating a few minutes to cook the peas. Serve over rice. Serves 4 to 6, depending on appetites.

Tuna or Chicken / Asparagus Supper

Assemble this dish ahead of time, then pop it into the oven at dinnertime — nice enough for company. Serve a salad, homemade crackers or bread, and a simple dessert such as fresh fruit or ice cream.

* * *

3 c. cooked rice
2 cans tuna, drained, *or* 2 c. chicken, cooked and chopped
1 can cream of chicken soup
$^1/_2$ c. sour cream *or* plain yogurt
$^1/_3$ c. onion, chopped
1 clove garlic, minced
Salt and pepper to taste
1 can asparagus pieces, drained
1 c. Cheddar cheese, grated

Combine everything except the cheese. Spoon into a 9x13x2-inch Pyrex dish, cover with foil, and bake at 350° F. for 30 minutes or until hot and bubbly. Top with cheese, and stick it back into the oven briefly to melt the cheese. Serves 4 or 5.

Southern Chicken Supper

Excellent to serve the family or guests, or to "tote" to a church supper. Assemble the casserole ahead of time and bake when needed.

* * *

2 c. cooked chicken, chopped
3 c. wide egg noodles, cooked
1/2 c. celery, chopped
1/3 c. onion, chopped
1/3 c. green pepper, chopped
1 tbsp. pimiento, chopped
1/3 to 1/2 c. mayonnaise
1/2 c. milk
1 can cream of mushroom soup
1 c. Cheddar cheese, grated
1/2 c. sliced almonds (optional)

Combine all ingredients except almonds. Spoon into a greased two-quart casserole. Bake at 400° F. for 20 minutes. Remove from oven, and top with almonds, if desired. Bake 5 more minutes. Serves six.

When Henry and I got married back in 1968 I started keeping a hostess book in which I write down the names of guests, when they dined with us, and the menu. This notebook is helpful in that I can check back and not keep serving the same people the same dishes; and after over two decades the pages of my hostess book reveal some fascinating food trends, as well as memory-joggers concerning old friends and special occasions. (You can also record preferences of guests, and even make note of the table setting, and your outfit!)

Pizzazz Parmesan Chicken

On the average, I test one new recipe per day, and also re-test other recipes. The Japanese have a proverb, "Eating a new food increases life expectancy by sixty days." My family and I should all live to be quite ancient!

Providentially, I married a man who is not necessarily the "meat and potatoes type." By that I mean that Henry does not have to have an easily-recognizable cut of red meat (steak, chop, prime rib) and a spud on his plate. He has always been adventurous enough to try casseroles, sauces, soups, stews, etc., with unknown (to him) ingredients; and he has no strong food dislikes. Both Henry and the children are valiant about plunging their forks into new dishes with optimism and enthusiasm. Pizzazz Parmesan Chicken immediately met their approval, without any modifications.

* * *

4 pieces uncooked chicken
2 c. canned tomato sauce
$^1/_4$ tsp. garlic powder
2 tbsp. Parmesan cheese
Mozzarella cheese, grated
Spaghetti noodles (We like whole wheat spaghetti noodles — better nutrition and flavor.)

Place the chicken parts in a foil-lined pan. Mix together tomato sauce, garlic powder, and Parmesan cheese. Pour over chicken. Cover pan with foil and bake at 375° F. for one hour. Remove foil, baste with sauce and bake 15 minutes more. Pour off chicken fat (but not the sauce!) and sprinkle with mozzarella cheese. Serve over cooked spaghetti noodles. — Thatsa some delish!

Don't Peek Baked Chicken

Have to be away almost all afternoon? This uncomplicated entree will come in handy. Just assemble the ingredients, slip the dish into the oven, and go on about your business. With no attention whatsoever, the main course for dinner cooks nicely. Add a simple fruit salad or a seasonal raw veggie salad, and dessert (cookies always bring smiles), and there's din-din.

* * *

1 can cream of mushroom soup
1 can cream of celery soup
1 c. converted rice, uncooked
1 ½ c. milk
4 or 5 pieces of cut-up, uncooked chicken
½ envelope dry onion soup mixture

Mix together the first four ingredients. Spoon into a 9x13x2-inch Pyrex baking dish. Place chicken parts on top of soup/rice mixture. Sprinkle with dry onion soup mix. Cover dish securely with foil, and bake at 300° F. for 3 hours, or at 325° F. for 2 ½ hours. Don't peek!

A word to the wise: A recent survey of National Merit Scholars was conducted to determine key factors which accounted for the success of these youngsters. Of the many characteristics considered, such as family income, study habits, school size, etc., it was discovered that high-achieving students had this in common: a daily, uninterrupted dinner hour with their family, at which time there was conversation about the day's activities.

Citrus Grove Baked Chicken

A good family dinner might include this "split-personality" dish which can go lemon-y or orange-y.

* * *

Uncooked chicken pieces for 4 to 6

2 cans cream of mushroom soup
2 tsp. grated lemon peel *or* orange peel
¼ c. lemon juice *or* orange juice
¼ c. onion, minced
½ tsp. basil
½ tsp. oregano

Cooked rice (preferably brown)
Parsley
Paprika

    Place the chicken parts in a baking dish. In a bowl, combine the next six ingredients. Pour over chicken. Bake uncovered at 375° F. for 1 hour and 15 minutes or until tender. Garnish with parsley and dust with paprika. Serve over rice.

Unflappable Chicken Dijon

"Hassle-free" and so-o-o-o good . . . .

* * *

4 to 5 pieces uncooked chicken

2 cans cream of chicken soup
3 tbsp. Dijon mustard (or spicy brown mustard)
$\frac{1}{2}$ tsp. oregano
$\frac{1}{4}$ tsp. black pepper
$\frac{1}{2}$ c. dry white wine *or* sherry

Cooked rice (preferably brown)

    Place the chicken in a large baking pan. Mix the next five ingredients and pour over the fowl. Bake uncovered at 375° F. for an hour or until tender. Serve over rice.

Sarah's Casserole

    My daughter Sarah Evangeline Mitchell dictated (from the bathtub!) this superb recipe to me when she was not quite three years old. — Needless to say, I enjoy cooking and spend a lot of time in the kitchen. Sarah seems to be following in my footsteps.

* * *

3 c. wide egg noodles, cooked
1 c. canned or cooked corn, drained
$1\frac{1}{2}$ c. cooked broccoli, chopped

1$\frac{1}{2}$ c. cooked chicken, chopped
Salt and pepper, if desired
1 can cream of mushroom soup
1 can cream of chicken soup

Combine all ingredients and bake in a casserole dish at 350° F. for approximately 30 minutes, or until bubbly. Serves 3 or 4.

Delores Motley's Chicken Pie

One afternoon at the Pittsylvania County public library where I do much of my foodwriting research the ladies were raving about a dish someone had brought in for their "communal" lunch. Naturally I asked for the recipe, and here it is.

* * *

1 tbsp. butter *or* margarine
1 c. onion, chopped
1 c. celery, chopped

1 can cream of chicken soup
1$\frac{1}{2}$ c. milk
$\frac{1}{4}$ tsp. garlic powder
$\frac{1}{4}$ tsp. black pepper
3 c. cooked, cubed chicken
2$\frac{1}{2}$ oz. jar sliced mushrooms, drained
1 c. frozen green peas

1 can Hungry Jack Biscuits (10 biscuits in the can); cut each
      biscuit into fourths
$\frac{1}{4}$ c. Parmesan cheese
1 tbsp. sesame seeds

Sauté the onion and celery in butter or margarine. (To save time and calories, you can omit the butter or margarine and sautéing.) Add the next seven ingredients and heat until bubbly. Pour this mixture into an ungreased 8- or 9-inch square baking dish. At this point mix the Parmesan cheese and sesame seeds and coat the biscuit quarters with this mixture. Arrange the biscuits over the chicken mixture and sprinkle on any remaining cheese and seed coating mixture. Bake at 375° F. for 15 to 20 minutes. Serves 6.

Note: For a variation, mashed potatoes could be used for the topping.

The next two recipes produce emergency-fast meals.

Hurry Curry

Chopped chicken, chopped turkey, or tuna can be used.

* * *

$^1/_4$ c. onion, chopped
1 can cream of mushroom soup
$^1/_4$ c. sour cream *or* yogurt
$^1/_2$ tsp. curry powder
1 c. chopped chicken, chopped turkey, *or* tuna

Rice *or* noodles, cooked

Heat together the first five ingredients. Meanwhile, prepare rice or noodles. Serve Hurry Curry over rice or noodles, sprinkled with paprika for a pretty dash of color. Serve with a salad or vegetable, and dessert.

Monterey Tuna Treat

Tired and hungry? Put on some rice to cook, open a can, and supper is almost ready. Read on!

* * *

1 can tuna, undrained
2 onions, sliced

2 to 3 c. cooked rice (white rice tastes better in this recipe, though brown rice is more healthful)
1 c. Monterey Jack or mozzarella cheese, grated

Cook the tuna and onions together, covered, until the onions are soft. Dump in the rice and cheese. Stir until everything is warm and melty. Yummy! Enough for a cozy twosome for dinner.

Poultry Pasta Parmigiana

1 or 2 cans cream of chicken soup (depending on how rich you want the dish to taste)
$1/2$ c. water, milk, *or* chicken broth
$1/3$ c. onion, chopped
$3/4$ c. red and green pepper, cut in strips
2 c. cooked, chopped chicken (*or* turkey)
$1/4$ c. Parmesan cheese
Black pepper

2 tbsp. dry sherry *or* white wine
Spaghetti noodles, cooked

Combine the first seven ingredients in a saucepan, and cook covered for 15 minutes, stirring occasionally. Stir in sherry. Serve over hot cooked spaghetti noodles. Produces 4 to 5 servings.

The next recipe is a favorite of my hustand's.

Romanesque Simmered Chicken

4 or 5 pieces uncooked chicken
1 onion, sliced

2 cloves garlic, minced
2 c. canned tomatoes
Salt to taste
A few grindings of black pepper
$1/2$ tsp. oregano
$1/4$ c. dry white or rosé wine, *or* dry sherry

Cooked rice (preferably brown)

In a large pot combine everything except the wine. Heat to boiling; stir; reduce heat and simmer covered for an hour, or until the chicken is tender. (Stir occasionally.) Add wine, and check the seasonings. Serve over rice. (We are "rice-aholics!")

You'll notice that some of the recipes in this cookbook are less complicated or time-consuming to prepare than others. (Some have fewer than half a dozen ingredients.) Most people have extremely tight schedules during the work-week (and often meetings, church, etc., at night), so on those nights you need to pick out one of the super simple recipes. Hopefully on the weekend, though, things loosen up a little, allowing more kitchen time. Then you can select some of the slightly more complex recipes and those requiring advance preparation. (You can always refrigerate or freeze casseroles made during the weekend to use on work days.)

Chicken Cacciatore

2 c. (one 16- or 17-ounce can) tomatoes
4 pieces chicken
1 medium onion, chopped or sliced (sliced looks prettier)
1 clove garlic, minced
1 tsp. basil
1 tbsp. dried parsley
$1/4$ c. dry sherry *or* white wine
Salt and pepper

Cooked rice (preferably brown)

Combine the ingredients in a pot. Bring to a simmer, cover, and cook about an hour (until tender). Serve over rice.

Danish Chicken

The secret of this delicious and imaginative dish — a "regular" on my menus for over twenty years — is in the sauce, predominantly flavored by curry powder and tomato. Our neighbor Eloise Folkers Nenon, whose ancestry is Nordic, originated and named this entree, which I have since modified. When we lived in New Orleans I bought the curry powder for Danish Chicken at the tiny Flavorworld herb and spice shop on St. Ann Street just off Jackson Square in the French Quarter . . . . Our friend Jack R. Miller, famed New Orleans printmaker, dubbed the dish "Dangerous Chicken" when he first tasted it because it's so exotic with unknown elements and, to the uninitiated, startling flavors. Suggested accompaniments: a tossed salad with blue cheese dressing; Apple Betty for dessert.

* * *

4 pieces of chicken, stewed until just tender
2 tbsp. oil *or* margarine
$^1/_2$ c. onion, chopped
1 tsp. curry powder
1 tsp. paprika
$^1/_4$ tsp. salt
2 tbsp. flour
$^1/_2$ c. water (*or* broth from cooking chicken)
$^1/_2$ c. tomato sauce

Cooked rice (preferably brown)
Parsley for garnish

Prepare the sauce by cooking the onion in the oil or margarine until the onion becomes tender and translucent. Add seasonings. Blend in flour and let it cook for a few minutes, stirring well. Add water and tomato sauce, and heat until smooth and thick. Remove sauce from stove and pour over cooked chicken pieces. Refrigerate overnight, so that the poultry absorbs the flavors and the sauce mellows.

When you are ready to serve Danish Chicken, cook enough rice for four people, and heat the Danish Chicken. Mound rice on each plate, and on the bed of rice place a piece of chicken. Then spoon on the sauce and serve garnished with parsley.

Rondo Chicken Delight

Cherished recipes gleaned from the files of family and friends have enhanced tremendously my "meal offerings." The following entry, Rondo Chicken Delight, was served to my husband and me in the home of Lanier and Mary Gail Easley of Rondo, Virginia, a small community located between Chatham and Martinsville. Despite its ease of preparation, this "epitome of simplicity" recipe is a lovely and rather fancy dinner entree.

* * *

8 chicken breasts, de-boned
$^1/_2$ lb. sliced bacon
1 c. sour cream
1 pkg. dried chipped beef
1 can cream of mushroom soup

Lightly grease a large, shallow Pyrex baking dish. Wrap chicken breasts in bacon. Line baking dish with dried beef. Mix sour cream with soup and pour over chicken. Cover and bake for 3 hours at 300° F. Serves eight.

By the time we had lived in New Orleans awhile we knew enough about food to operate a small French Quarter restaurant for a friend, and later to write restaurant critiques and articles for a magazine we published there.

In the position of magazine writers/reporters Henry and I had the grand opportunity to be invited into various

Creole/Cajun/French kitchens, where the chefs would let us "peek into their pots!" Now, that was a culinary learning experience!

After collecting recipes for such a long time, I have even forgotten where I got some of my "oldie goldies." Friends give me lots of recipes, and, of course, I test and develop my own. Over the years, some "favorites" are superseded by a "more favorite" group of ingredients or method of preparation, based on our changing tastes and nutritional awareness. Some early favorites still appear on our weekly menus, though. They are definitely "tried and true" after all this time.

Those reminiscences bring to mind Graham Kerr, the Galloping Gourmet, our TV hero back in the early 1970's. Do you remember how Kerr could mince veggies with lightning speed and precision, talk a mile a minute, and all the while juggle a glass of wine? What fabulous-looking dishes he pulled from the oven! And then he'd invite a lady from the audience to sit at a little elegantly-set table with him to sample the food.

*Because I was such a fan of his, of course I tuned in to see his guest appearance on **The Phil Donahue Show** on November 11, 1975. How surprised I was to hear him tell about accepting Jesus Christ as his Lord and Saviour! Both Henry and I had been considering the claims of Jesus after reading Catherine Marshall's book **Something More**. Kerr's witness was the clincher! Henry had to get out of the bathtub, wrapped in a towel, to come in and see the last part of Donahue's show, at which time the Galloping Gourmet told viewers how to pray to receive Christ into their lives. We prayed, and received.*

Broccoli-Chicken Délicieux

My mother developed this "may I have the recipe?" recipe. You will be most pleased with the taste, texture, and appearance of this uncomplicated, yet sophisticated, entree.

* * *

2 pkg. frozen broccoli spears, cooked and drained
6 chicken breasts, stewed, skinned, de-boned, and sliced
2 cans cream of chicken soup
$\frac{1}{4}$ c. sherry *or* $\frac{1}{4}$ c. liquid from cooking broccoli
$\frac{1}{2}$ c. Cheddar cheese, grated
Additional cheese for topping, and buttered bread crumbs *or*
    canned French-fried onions

Arrange broccoli spears and sliced chicken in a greased 9x13x2-inch baking dish. Mix soup, $\frac{1}{4}$ c. liquid, and $\frac{1}{2}$ c. cheese. Pour over chicken and broccoli. If you opt for bread crumbs and more cheese, put them on before baking. (Otherwise, add the French-fried onions the last 5 minutes of baking time.) Bake the casserole at 350° F. for 40 minutes.

Texarkana Range-Top Chicken

Not bland, this happy mixture will make your taste buds stand up on tippy-toe. One of my favorites!

* * *

$2\frac{1}{2}$ c. canned tomatoes, cut-up, and some of their liquid
$\frac{1}{2}$ c. onion, chopped
$\frac{1}{2}$ c. green pepper, chopped
2 cloves garlic, minced
1 tbsp. chili powder (or less to suit your taste)

1 to 2 cups chopped cooked chicken
2 c. whole kernel corn
Salt and pepper

Cooked rice (preferably brown)

In a large pot simmer together the first five ingredients for around 15 minutes; then add the next three ingredients and cook a few more minutes. Serve over rice. Serves 4 to 6.

Pitt Barbecue Sauce

We live in Chatham, Virginia, in Pittsylvania County, places named in honor of 1700's English politician William Pitt, Earl of Chatham. The following sauce is distinguished on chicken. (Cover the chicken with sauce and bake at 375° F. for 60 to 75 minutes or until tender, basting occasionally.)

* * *

Mix the following ingredients:

1 1/4 c. canned tomato sauce
1/3 c. onion, minced
1/4 c. vinegar
1 tbsp. brown sugar
1 tbsp. prepared mustard
2 tbsp. bottled steak sauce

Aplenty Barbecue Sauce

4 c. canned tomato sauce
1/3 c. lemon juice
1/4 c. Worcestershire sauce
1/4 c. honey
2 tbsp. molasses
2 tbsp. vinegar
1 1/2 tsp. Texas Pete *or* similar liquid red pepper seasoning
1 clove garlic, minced
1/2 c. onion, chopped

Mix all ingredients. (If preparing chicken, simply pour over chicken pieces and bake as suggested in the previous recipe.)

Simple 'n' Satisfying Barbecued Chicken

People have complimented me on this dish, so it must taste more difficult to prepare than it is. In fact, nothing could be easier! We enjoy Simple 'n' Satisfying Barbecued Chicken with Four Bean Salad or a tossed salad, Irish or sweet potatoes, and fresh fruit and cheese for dessert (or homemade cake or pie, if time permits):

* * *

Line a baking pan with aluminum foil. Place chicken parts in the pan and pour bottled barbecue sauce on each piece of poultry. Bake uncovered at 350° F. for 1 hour and 15 minutes; during that time pour on additional sauce once or twice. If the chicken begins to brown too rapidly, cover with foil.

A funny "kitchen drama" occurred when I forgot to put the ground beef in the bean mixture for chili, but a recent cooking booboo really "takes the cake" . . . .

As I mentioned, I test as many as five or six new recipes a week (averaging one new one per day). On those days when I'm really in the cooking mood and mode I might have a new bread recipe at all three meals, a new main course at lunch and/or dinner, and a new salad dressing, vegetable dish, or dessert to boot. (I also re-test many recipes.) I have all of these recipes written out on index cards. When I'm in a "cooking frenzy" these cards and the ingredients clutter my kitchen work area.

Not long ago I had clipped out a magazine recipe for a barley/black-eyed pea marinated salad that looked promising. I made some changes in the recipe to better suit my ideas of taste and nutrition and jotted down my modified list of ingredients on a card. I failed to clip the original recipe with the title and instructions onto my index card. When I got around to testing the dish I glibly cooked the barley, added everything else and before too long served this "vegetarian entree" to my hungry crew. We decided the dish was "so-so." — Imagine my surprise when, later on, I went to make my usual notes about the recipe on the card, and discovered the original recipe: "Cover and refrigerate salad until chilled . . . ."

Autumn Chicken and Barley Medley

This is a visually beautiful dish.

* * *

In a large pot combine:

1 c. raw barley
3 to 4 c. chicken broth
4 pieces chicken (previously stewed until just barely tender)
$\frac{1}{2}$ c. onion, chopped
1 c. canned tomatoes, chopped
2 tsp. curry powder
$1\frac{1}{2}$ tsp. dry parsley
1 tsp. sage
$\frac{1}{2}$ tsp. garlic powder
Salt and pepper to taste

Cook 40 minutes covered, checking and stirring occasionally. — Add water if mixture gets too dry.

Italian Country Casserole

This dish is a snap to fix, once you've got the chopped, cooked chicken. (I stew chickens ahead of time, chop up the meat, and freeze it in one-cup portions to use later in casseroles, stews, and soups. You can skip that, and buy canned chopped chicken.) As you can see, previously-cooked rice is necessary, too, but at our household of rice addicts, I prepare enough to accumulate plenty of left-over rice.

* * *

2 c. cooked chicken, chopped
2 c. canned tomatoes, chopped (undrained)
2 c. cooked rice
$\frac{1}{4}$ c. onion, chopped finely

2 tbsp. pimiento-stuffed olives, chopped
¼ tsp. salt
¼ tsp. thyme
American or Cheddar cheese, grated

Combine all ingredients except the cheese. Spoon into an oven-to-table casserole dish. Cover and bake at 375° F. for 30 minutes, or until hot and bubbly. Sprinkle liberally with cheese and serve. (We enjoy baked potatoes as a side dish.)

Chicken Livers Paprika

Delicious — you'll vote for this one!

* * *

2 tbsp. oil, butter *or* margarine
1 c. onions, thinly sliced
1 lb. chicken livers, drained
¼ tsp. salt
1½ tsp. paprika
¼ c. sour cream

Sauté the onion in the oil until just tender. Add livers, and cook briefly, stirring once. Season, and fold in the sour cream. Serves three or four, depending upon how enthusiastic (and hungry) your liver-eaters are.

The following recipes put me in mind of a "traumatic" food experience I had involving Italian food. When I was in elementary school the "lunch room" was in a separate building behind the red brick schoolhouse. (The lunch room was actually a converted Victorian house.) We children filed through the hall of the old house and picked up our milk and then our plate lunches. I always got "white" milk — I thought of chocolate milk as a treat/dessert-type beverage, not as a suitable accompaniment to a meal — but one day the white milk was all gone when I came to the refrigerated chest! I had to take a carton of chocolate milk. I proceeded to get my plate lunch. It was spaghetti. Soon my teacher discovered me crying pitifully. Upon interrogating me, she ascertained that to my first-grade mind and palate the thought of chocolate milk and spaghetti was sickening. I thought they clashed. (I still do.) The idea of eating such a meal had depressed me to tears! My teacher, noble and understanding lady that she was, traded her white milk for my chocolate. Happiness was restored. — Eat the following dishes, and be happy!

Bessie Payne's Spaghetti Sauce

Bessie Payne of Chatham is the mother of my friend since tot-hood, Ginger Payne Ripley. Mrs. Payne has been preparing this tummy-tempting spaghetti sauce for decades. (Little girls *and* big girls love it!) Now, if an Italian saw this recipe, he might blanch — "Catsup?!" But if he TASTED it, he'd be pleasantly surprised. (I have successfully substituted canned tomato sauce for the catsup . . . .)

* * *

1 lb. ground beef, crumbled, cooked, and drained
2 large onions, chopped
2 green peppers, chopped
1 qt. tomatoes and juice
1 tbsp. sugar
1 tsp. salt (or less to suit taste)
Dash of pepper
2 c. catsup (*or* canned tomato sauce)

Combine everything. Simmer, covered, for 2 hours. Serve over spaghetti noodles, and pass the Parmesan cheese.

When I was scarcely more than a toddler, my parents decided that it was time to bid adieu to the old Hotpoint stove (the kind on legs). I can remotely remember sitting, hunched over, under the stove and sobbing when I heard that it was "going bye-bye." Mom says that I expressed to her that I did not want them to get rid of it because I did not think that the food would taste right if it were cooked on another stove. She inquired specifically (probably just to try to humor me), "Which food would not be as good?" I responded, "Spaghetti." The only spaghetti Mom ever prepared was heated right out of the can!

My own current short-cut spaghetti? Brown and drain some ground beef. Meanwhile, heat a large bottle of commercial spaghetti sauce with mushrooms. Stir the cooked meat into the heated sauce. Serve over spaghetti noodles. Pass the Parmesan. Delightfully easy and good!

The Easiest Lasagna Recipe You Ever Saw

8 lasagna noodles, cooked
2 c. cottage cheese
1 $\frac{1}{2}$ c. mozzarella cheese, shredded
2 $\frac{1}{4}$ c. canned tomato sauce
$\frac{1}{2}$ lb. ground beef, crumbled, cooked, and drained

Using a 13x9x2-inch baking dish make layers: noodles, cottage cheese, mozzarella cheese, then tomato sauce and meat. Repeat. Bake at 375° F. for 30 minutes. Let stand 10 minutes.

The Fastest Lasagna Recipe You Ever Saw
(No Baking)

$\frac{1}{2}$ lb. ground beef, crumbled, cooked, and drained
1 lg. can (about 30 oz.) spaghetti sauce with mushrooms

$^1/_4$ c. onion, chopped
$^1/_4$ c. green pepper, chopped (optional)
$^1/_4$ c. Parmesan cheese
1 tsp. basil
1 tsp. oregano
6 cooked lasagna noodles, cut in half, *or* 3 c. dry egg noodles,
      cooked, *or* other pasta of your choosing
$^1/_2$ c. cottage cheese

1 c. mozzarella cheese

    Combine everything except the mozzarella cheese in a large pot. Heat, and simmer together 30 minutes. To serve, put half of the mixture in a serving dish. Top with $^1/_2$ c. mozzarella cheese. Pour in remaining sauce/noodle mixture. Top with $^1/_2$ c. mozzarella. Makes 4 to 6 servings.

Mad Russian's Hamburger Stroganoff

    When you come "madly rushin' " into the kitchen, here's a recipe for fast results. Count Paul Stroganoff, the Czarist Russian diplomat for whom such dishes are named, would be pleased with your ability to stir things up quickly!

    During June 1969 Harry and Cathy Yeatts moved next door to us at Draper's Meadow Apartments in Blacksburg. Although we all shared rather meager circumstances, they were the first people (other than Henry's relatives) to invite us to dinner. Cathy prepared Hamburger Stroganoff, which we ate sitting on the floor, with cardboard boxes for tables. A Chianti bottle/melted wax "candle-holder" helped to illuminate the room. The meal was hearty, the companionship sweet. Hamburger Stroganoff is still a favorite of ours . . . .

* * *

$^3/_4$ to 1 lb. ground beef, or less if you prefer
$^1/_2$ c. onion, chopped

$^1/_8$ tsp. garlic powder
1 can cream of mushroom soup
$^1/_4$ c. plain yogurt *or* sour cream (we use yogurt)
Broad egg noodles, cooked
Paprika
Parsley sprigs

Sauté the meat. Drain off the fat. Put the onion, garlic powder, mushroom soup, and yogurt into the saucepan with the beef and cook on medium low heat about 20 minutes. Meanwhile, prepare enough noodles for each plate and top with Stroganoff. Sprinkle with paprika and decorate each serving with a parsley sprig.

Romanov's Ground Beef Stroganoff

Romanov, of course, is the family name of Russia's royalty, in whose service Paul Stroganoff strove.

As the name indicates, this Stroganoff is fancier than Mad Russian's Hamburger Stroganoff, and would be quite suitable to serve guests.

* * *

1 lb. ground beef
$^1/_2$ c. onion, chopped
$^1/_2$ tsp. garlic powder
2 tbsp. flour
1 tsp. salt (or less, to suit your taste)
$^1/_4$ tsp. black pepper
$^1/_4$ tsp. paprika
1 small can of mushroom stems and pieces, drained
1 can cream of chicken soup
1 c. sour cream
Chives
Broad egg noodles, cooked

Cook together the meat and the onion, and drain off the grease (I use an iron skillet for this step). Combine in a saucepan the meat-onion mixture, seasonings, mushrooms, soup, and sour cream. Heat thoroughly, but do not boil. To serve, spoon Romanov's Ground Beef Stroganoff onto cooked egg noodles and sprinkle with chopped chives. Serves four to six.

Cheeseburger Pie

Longtime friend and top-notch cook Judy Boswell of Chatham contributed the next selection.

* * *

1 (8-oz.) pkg. crescent rolls

1 lb. ground beef

2 tbsp. instant minced onion
1 (8-oz.) can tomato sauce
4 oz. sliced mushrooms
1 (16-oz.) can green beans, drained
$^1/_4$ tsp. garlic salt
$^1/_4$ tsp. salt
$^1/_8$ tsp. pepper

1 egg, beaten
2 c. shredded cheese

Press rolls into an ungreased 9-inch pie plate to form crust. Brown beef and drain well. Add next seven ingredients and simmer for 15 minutes. Remove from heat. Stir egg into meat mixture and pour over crust in the pie plate. Top with cheese. Bake at 325° F. for 30 to 40 minutes, or until the center is firm.

Tip-Top Pan-Broiled Meat Loaves

This is a family-pleaser of over a decade . . . .

* * *

1 lb. ground beef
1 egg, beaten (optional)
$\frac{1}{8}$ tsp. oregano
$\frac{1}{8}$ tsp. black pepper
$\frac{1}{8}$ tsp. garlic powder
$\frac{1}{4}$ tsp. salt
$\frac{1}{4}$ c. quick oatmeal (uncooked)
$\frac{1}{4}$ c. dry milk powder
1 tbsp. onion, minced
2 tbsp. fresh celery leaves, minced (optional)

$\frac{3}{4}$ c. canned tomato sauce

Combine the above ingredients (except for the tomato sauce). Shape into four loaves. Brown in a greased skillet, turning to brown both sides. Pour off fat. (Transfer meat loaves to a skillet which is not iron, if you browned them in an iron skillet, as I do. The reason is that the iron affects the color of the tomato sauce which you add next.) Pour canned tomato sauce over the meat. Cover, lower the heat, and simmer for 20 minutes. Serves four.

. . . A Word About Steak . . .

Talking about beef, at my first (and last!) invitation to dine at friend Betty Toler's house, I was quite impressed to be served steak. (We did not have steak at home.) Thinking of an appropriate compliment, I announced to Mrs. Toler that the steak was so tender I could cut it with a fork. As I proceeded to demonstrate this fact, the steak jumped off my plate and onto the snow-white linen tablecloth. Ugh!

And any steak recipe reminds me of the "Great Steak Weekend" Henry and I experienced while in college, the year before we married.

Tired from a week of classes and hungry from trying to subsist on terrible dining-hall food, we decided to reward ourselves at Saturday noon with charboiled-to-perfection 16-oz. T-bone steaks at the great local Farmhouse Restaurant. Then a dinner invitation from sympathetic cousin Marguerite Gunn netted us Pepper Steak in a lovingly-prepared Oriental-style meal. ("At least it was different from All-American-slab-of-meat-steak.")

*Stuffed, we slept late (in our respective dormitories) and skipped breakfasts on Sunday, then dropped into the Hardy House Restaurant for their $1.49 luncheon special, usually spaghetti or fried fish or chicken, but today — 12-oz. **broiled T-bone steak**! "We're certainly glad," we agreed, eating slowly, "that our dinner invitation tonight (another helpful cousin) is for Shrimp Creole."*

*No such luck. The menu was changed. "I remembered how much college students love steak," commented Lois Carr as she swept out of the kitchen with **a huge platter of broiled steaks**. ("Is something wrong? . . . No seconds? . . . Who's going to eat all this steak?!")*

Anyway, the following Oven Swiss Steak is an old-timey favorite for your meat-and-potatoes fans.

Old-Fashioned Oven Swiss Steak

Remember when steak was used to *celebrate* something? I recall steaks on the Fourth of July at Smith Mountain Lake (Virginia), before the fireworks display began; fabulous Beef Fondue dinner parties in New Orleans; "special occasion" college-days steak dinners at the Farmhouse Restaurant in Blacksburg; and the annual Christmas steak dinner at Hargrave

Military Academy (where my parents worked), the high point of the year, with dimmed lights, twinkling Christmas tree, beautifully-appointed long tables, and hot, thick, sizzling, juicy steaks. Here's a recipe to stir or create warm, homey memories:

* * *

$1^{1}/_{2}$ lb. beef round steak
$^{1}/_{4}$ c. flour
$^{1}/_{4}$ to $^{1}/_{2}$ tsp. salt
1 (16-oz.) can stewed tomatoes
$^{1}/_{2}$ c. celery, chopped
$^{1}/_{2}$ c. carrot, chopped
2 tbsp. onion, chopped
$^{1}/_{2}$ tsp. Worcestershire sauce
$^{1}/_{4}$ c. Cheddar cheese, grated

Cut the meat into four portions. Mix the flour and salt, and pound into the meat (setting aside the extra flour and salt mixture). Brown the meat in a small amount of oil or shortening, and then place the meat in a shallow baking dish. Blend the remaining flour and salt with the drippings in the skillet, and add the other ingredients (except cheese). Cook this skillet mixture, stirring constantly, until it boils. Pour over meat. Cover and bake at 350° F. for two hours. Top with cheese and heat a few additional minutes. Serves four.

Burgundy Beef Casserole

Jane Cox, who now lives in Atlanta, Georgia, gave me this recipe when we were Air Force wives in Dayton, Ohio. — As this casserole cooks, a savory gravy forms . . . . That reminds of a cute quote from singer Naomi Judd. She remarked, "[Mama] put gravy on everything but our shoes."

* * *

1 lb. lean beef chuck, cut into 1½-inch cubes
½ tsp. salt
⅛ tsp. pepper
1 small onion, sliced
½ c. red wine (dry Burgundy)
1 can beef consommé
¼ c. flour
¼ c. dry bread crumbs

Rice *or* noodles, cooked

Put beef into a greased casserole dish. In a separate bowl, mix wine, seasonings, consommé, and onion; and then stir in flour and bread crumbs. Pour this mixture over the beef. Bake covered at 300° F. for three hours. Serve over rice or noodles. Serves three or four.

Talking about gravy, when I was a little girl we often had roast beef for the Sunday midday meal. (The roast cooked while we were at church, and Mom always worried about the house burning down.) To MY way of thinking, this roast beef was hard to cut, impossible to chew, stringy, and dry (a child's point of view — unskilled hands, baby teeth, small mouth). But I liked the "au jus" gravy! I loved a thick slice of Sunbeam Salt-Rising bread soaked with beef broth. I ate it with a fork. That with some mashed potatoes (plus a few string beans to please Mom) was very fine eating.

Yankee Doodle Noodle and Ham Bake

3 c. broad egg noodles, cooked
1½ c. cooked ham, chopped
1 can cream of chicken soup
1 c. Cheddar cheese, grated
2 tbsp. butter *or* margarine (optional)

Combine noodles, ham, and cheese. Put in a greased oven-to-table casserole dish. Dot with butter or margarine, if desired. Bake at 375° F. for 20 minutes. Serves 3 or 4.

Spring Garden Pork Chops

The carrots and green pepper in this medley contribute irresistible colors to the dish, and sage adds a whisper of mysterious flavor. We named Spring Garden Pork Chops in honor of Spring Garden, the community in which Henry grew up.

* * *

4 pork chops
Vegetable oil
1 can Campbell's Golden Mushroom Soup
$^1/_4$ c. water
$^1/_2$ c. onion, chopped
$^1/_2$ c. green pepper, chopped
1 c. carrots, thinly sliced
$^1/_4$ tsp. sage

Brown the pork chops in a skillet, using a small amount of oil. Pour off the fat. Stir in the remaining ingredients, and cover. Simmer 30 minutes (or until the chops are tender), stirring occasionally.

May all your meals be happy and not harried — low-stress and yet pleasurable. — Just take it easy and enjoy!